The Make Love With Life
Journal

Ken Vegotsky

AGES Publications™
Los Angeles, California, U.S.A. & Toronto,

Copyright © 1997 by Ken Vegotsky

How To Make Love With Life™
THE LOVE LIVING & LIVE LOVING SERIES™

The Make Love With Life Journal
1-886508-02-X
First printing 1997   10 9 8 7 6 5 4 3 2

Editor: Stephanie Vegotsky
Cover and Interior Design: Inside Bestsellers™
Manufactured in Canada

Adi, Gaia, Esalen Publications Inc.
8391 Beverly St. #323-ML,
Los Angeles, CA 90048

Contact coordinator (519) 396-9553

Quantity discounted orders are available for Groups.
Please make enquiries to Bulk Sales Department at the
above address.
Telephone orders 1 (800) 263-1991

The Make Love With Life
Journal

A Love Living and Live Loving Gift Book

Made so easy for you we've even included a time saving personal letter.
All you have to do is fill in the blanks or check off the appropriate
spaces. Then put it in an envelope that is at least 5 3/4 inches by 8 1/2
inches.

It can even be a gift you give yourself!

More than just a book, more than just a card - it's a gift, card, book and
journal all rolled up into one neat nifty package. Savoring memories and
saving time, is in part, what making love with life is all about.

Date _____

Dear _____

____Self   ___Girlfriend   ____Mom   ___Grandma

____Wife   ___Daughter   ____Granddaughter

____Friend   ___Co-worker

I glanced through this charming book, discovered it has lots of
space to write in and great inspirational and motivational sayings
that will enhance _____ my _____ your Making Love With Life Journal
experience.

Its compact size means _____ I _____ you can take it everywhere.
Never again will _____ I _____ you miss the opportunity to record a
special thought or precious moment.

It seemed like the perfect gift to give you for

____Valentines Day   ___Your birthday   ___Mothers Day

____Engagement gift   ___Hanukkah   ___Christmas

____Just being you… because your special.

other_____

You deserve more than just

____a card   ___a book   ____a journal

____this, but it's all I can afford, at this time.

Enjoy this tasty treat… at least it's not fattening. I remain,
sincerely yours

____With Love   ____Best Wishes

____Happy Holidays   ____Warmest Regards

Signed: _____

I dedicate this journal with a difference
to you, the reader.

May the inspirational and motivational sayings
nourish your mind, body and soul each day.

Savor the daily miracles and
the greatest of gifts called life.

Helping make your life
a richer and more rewarding experience,
makes this a better world,
one person at a time.

10 Tips to Enhance Your Journaling Experience

Discover the hidden jewels of your desires with your journaling experience. These guidelines are for your benefit, to stimulate and aid you. Use some, all or none of them as best suits your needs and feelings. They are aids to use as you see fit — leading you to uncovering the magical powers of your mind — helping you nourish your mind, body and soul.

Start where you are in your life now.

Don't keep secrets. They become hidden anchors to your inner and outer growth.

Write what you want and when you want it. Be clear. This gives your dreams a solid form, setting them in motion.

Follow through. Don't allow your inner critic to sabotage your efforts to create a richer and more rewarding life.

Write from the heart and tell the whole truth. This is a process of emerging gracefully from whatever trials and tribulations life throws your way — to discovering and delighting in your daily successes.

Ask yourself questions. Don't force the answers. Nourish your mind, body and soul by waiting patiently for the answers. The answers are within you.

If you get stuck, ask yourself this question: What is the truth at this moment?

Practice thankfulness, for the miraculous gifts of your life journey.

Practice forgiveness. This doesn't condone the actions of others. Forgiving another also means forgiving yourself. It enables you to let go and get on with life.

Create your own definition of success. Define yourself by who you are and your authentic inner voice. Savor each moment of your journey and
Make Love With Life!

Keep your face to the sunshine and
you cannot see the shadows.
Helen Keller

Love has a hundred gentle ends.

Leonora Speyer

To love oneself is the beginning of a
life-long romance.

Oscar Wilde

One cannot have wisdom without living life.

Dorothy McCall

E ach of us is recognized by the
   brilliance of our light.
                        Alice Bailey

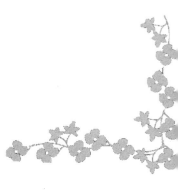

Love between two people is such a precious thing. It is not a possession.

I no longer need to possess to complete myself.
True love becomes my freedom.

Angela Wozniak

I look in the mirror through the eyes
of the child that was me.

Judy Collins

A complete reevaluation takes place in your physical and mental being when you've laughed and had some fun.

Catherine Ponder

Love is a great beautifier.

Louisa May Alcott

L ife's sweetest joys are hidden in
	unsubstantial things; an April
rain, a fragrance, a vision of blue wings.

Mary Riley Smith

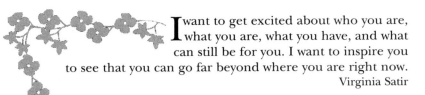

I want to get excited about who you are, what you are, what you have, and what can still be for you. I want to inspire you to see that you can go far beyond where you are right now.

Virginia Satir

Everything has its wonders, even
   darkness and silence, and I learn,
whatever state I may be in, therein to be content.
                                    Helen Keller

The future belongs to those who believe
in the beauty of their dreams.

Eleanor Roosevelt

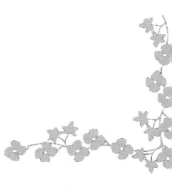

The only good luck many great
women ever had was being born
with the ability and determination to overcome bad luck.

Channing Pollock

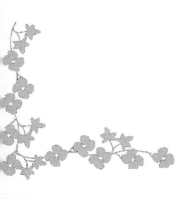

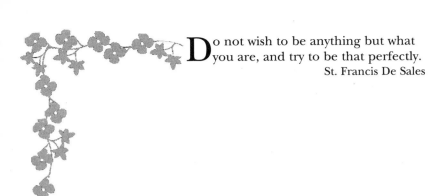

Do not wish to be anything but what you are, and try to be that perfectly.

St. Francis De Sales

Many receive advice, only the wise profit from it.

Syrus

Give and give infinitely.

G. Ohsawa

Heaven means to be one with God.

Confucius

Seek to know yourself and accept others.

Ken Vegotsky

We trek to every conceivable corner of consciousness and the planet in search of wholeness.
All along the answers lie deep within our own bodies.

Dr. Christiane Northrup

Whatever is flexible and flowing will
continue to grow;
whatever is rigid will tend to die.

Tao Te Ching

I shall never believe that God plays dice
with the world.

Albert Einstein

When you get into a tight place and
everything goes against you...
never give up then, for that is just the place and time that the
tide will turn.

Harriet Beecher Stowe

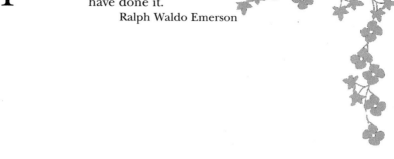

The reward of a thing well done is to have done it.

Ralph Waldo Emerson

Humor is an aphrodisiac for making love with life.

Ken Vegotsky

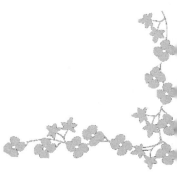

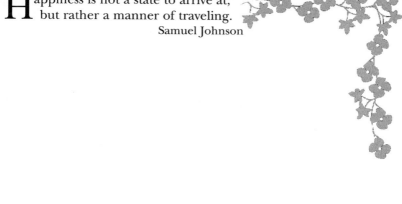

Happiness is not a state to arrive at,
but rather a manner of traveling.
Samuel Johnson

The highest reward for a person's toil is not what they get for it, but what they become by it.

J. Ruskin

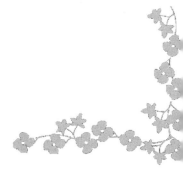

H ugs are a gentle form of healing massage.

Ken Vegotsky

Happiness lies in the joy of achievement and the thrill of creative effort.

Franklin Roosevelt

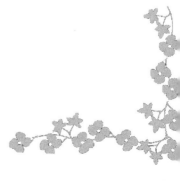

To love what you do and feel that it matters, how could anything be more fun?

Katherine Graham

You will become as small as your
controlling desire:
as great as your dominant aspiration.
James Allen

The person that makes the greatest mistake is one that hesitates to attempt changes for fear of making a mistake.

Lumir Victor Mika

The secret of happiness is not in doing what one likes, but in liking what one does.

James Barrie

If you look like your passport photo, in all probability you need the journey.

E. Wilson

A misty morning does not signify a cloudy day.

Ancient saying

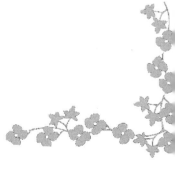

Far away – there in the sunshine are
my highest aspirations.
I may not reach them, but I can look up
and see their beauty, believe in them and try to follow where
they may lead.

Louisa May Alcott

To love for the sake of being loved is human. But to love for the sake of loving is angelic.

Alphonse de Lamartine

Fortunately psychoanalysis is not the
only way to resolve inner conflict.
Life itself still remains a very effective therapist.
Karen Horney

Each moment of life is as sacred as
that which goes before it and that
which comes after it.

Ken Vegotsky

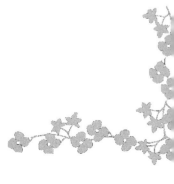

Only those who dare, truly live.

Ruth Freedman

L oving, like prayer, is a power as well
as a process.
It's curative. It is creative.

Zona Gale

The positive mind has extra problem-
solving power.

Author Unknown

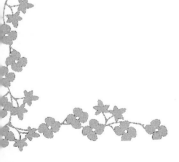

Yesterday is a canceled check;
    tomorrow a promissory note.
Today is the only cash you have.
        Spend it wisely.

Kay Lyons

B eing alive means you already are a winner, in the lottery of life.

Ken Vegotsky

L ove is not getting, but giving. It is
sacrifice. And sacrifice is glorious.
Joanna Field

L ove is like epidemic diseases. The more one fears it the more likely one is to contract it.

N. Chamfort

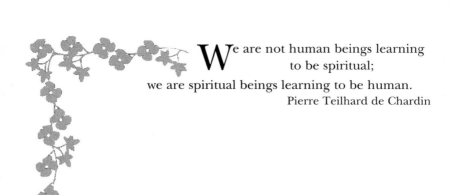

We are not human beings learning
to be spiritual;
we are spiritual beings learning to be human.

Pierre Teilhard de Chardin

Let the pooh-pooh of your past,
become fertilizer for your present,
so you can grow a new tomorrow, today.

Ken Vegotsky

Heaven is under our feet as well as
over our heads.
Henry David Thoreau

The greatest gift we can give one another is rapt attention to one another's existence.

Sue Ebaugh

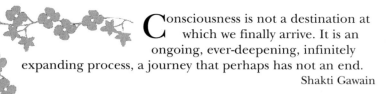

Consciousness is not a destination at which we finally arrive. It is an ongoing, ever-deepening, infinitely expanding process, a journey that perhaps has not an end.

Shakti Gawain

Life is too short to be little.

Disraeli

E mptiness is caused by the child
within going into hiding.

C. Whitfield

Genius is the ability to reduce the
complicated to the simple.

C. Ceran

Love living and live loving.

Ken Vegotsky

No problem can stand the assault of
sustained thinking.

Voltaire

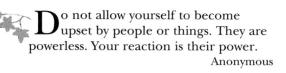

Do not allow yourself to become upset by people or things. They are powerless. Your reaction is their power.

Anonymous

A person will be just about as happy
as they make up their minds to be.

Abraham Lincoln

One is nearer God's heart in a garden.

D.F. Gurney

She who has conquered weakness, and has put way all selfish thoughts, belongs neither to oppressor nor oppressed. She is free.

James Allen

A great pleasure in life is doing what people say you cannot do.

W. Gagehot

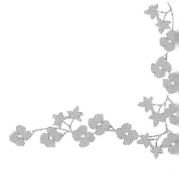

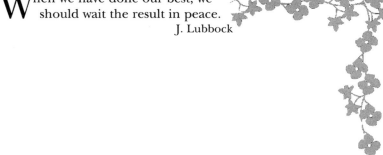

When we have done our best, we
should wait the result in peace.

J. Lubbock

Children are great teachers. Mine get me to practice the art of unconditional love, daily.

Ken Vegotsky

Failure is the opportunity to begin
again – more intelligently.
                              Henry Ford

L ove is in the air — it's up to me to catch the homeless kisses floating there.

Ken Vegotsky

A s I grow older, I pay less attention to what others say.
I just watch what they do.

Andrew Carnegie

The people who get on in this world are the people who get up and look for the circumstances they want, and if they can't find them, make them.

George Bernard Shaw

The best and most beautiful things in the world cannot be seen, not touched — but are felt in the heart.

Helen Keller

Love is the aphrodisiac of life.

Ken Vegotsky

Our life is frittered away by detail...Simplify, simplify.
Henry David Thoreau

Your living is determined not so much by what life brings you as by the attitude you bring to life.

J. Miller

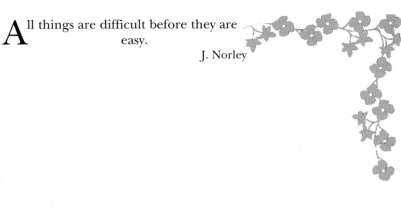

All things are difficult before they are easy.

J. Norley

People forget how fast you did a job, but they remember how well you did it.

Howard Newton

Our perceptions distort our reception.

Ken Vegotsky

There's no thrill in easy sailing when the skies are clear and blue, there's no joy in merely doing things which any one can do. But there is satisfaction that is mighty sweet to take, when you reach a destination that you thought you'd never make.

Spirella

Fate is what you make of it.

Ken Vegotsky

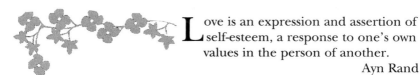

L ove is an expression and assertion of self-esteem, a response to one's own values in the person of another.

Ayn Rand

What happens to a woman is less significant than what happens within her.

Louis Mann

It takes two to speak the truth —
one to speak, and another to hear.

Henry David Thoreau

The symphony of life, is best heard in the silence between the notes. In fact in a real symphony it is the silences which make the music work best.

Ken Vegotsky

L ife is either a daring adventure or
    nothing at all.

Helen Keller

The dreamers are the saviors of the world.

James Allen

If it's to be, it's up to me.

Author Unknown

I perceive us to be spiritual beings. The human experience is the garden of our souls.

Ken Vegotsky

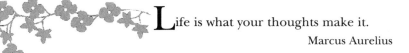

Life is what your thoughts make it.

Marcus Aurelius

The pessimist sees difficulty in every opportunity. The optimist sees opportunity in every difficulty.

Winston Churchill

M an is the only animal that blushes... Or needs to.

Mark Twain

I do the very best I know how, the very best I can, and I mean to keep on doing it to the end. If the end brings me out all right, what is said against me will not amount to anything. If the end brings me out all wrong, ten angels swearing I was right would make no difference.

Abraham Lincoln

I think I shall never see
A poem as lovely as a tree.

A. Joyce Kilmer

Those who bring sunshine to the lives of others cannot keep it from themselves.

J. Barrie

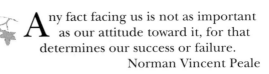

Any fact facing us is not as important as our attitude toward it, for that determines our success or failure.

Norman Vincent Peale

Things turn out the best for the people who make the best of the way things turn out.

J. Wooden

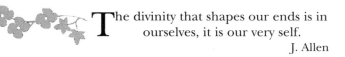

The divinity that shapes our ends is in ourselves, it is our very self.

J. Allen

I wake up in the morning, that's enough for me. The rest of the day is a bonus.

Ken Vegotsky

If our reach does not exceed our grasp
 – then why is there a heaven?

R. Browning

Two people look out through the same bars; one sees the mud and one the stars.

F. Langbridge

A chip on the shoulder indicates that
there is wood higher up.

J. Herbert

It is a funny thing about life - if you refuse to accept anything but the best, you very often get it.

Somerset Maugham

The rare and beautiful experiences of divine revelation are moments of special gifts. Each of us, however, lives each day with special gifts which are a part of our very being, and life is a process of discovering and developing these God-given gifts within each one of us.

Jeane Dixon

Use what talents you possess. the woods would be very silent if no birds sang there except those that sang best.

H. Dyke

An ounce of love is worth a pound of knowledge.

J. Wesley

L ove doesn't just sit there like a stone.
It has to be made, like brick: remade
all the time, made new.

Ursula K. LeGuin

K nowledge is gained by learning;
trust by doubt; and love by love.

T. Szasz

Make Love With Life!

Ken Vegotsky

From AGES Publications

Books

+

Audio Tapes

The Ultimate Power

An eight cassette audio tape program. Includes the book as a reference manual. Good as an aid for study groups or oneself.

Hypnotic Journey of Gentle Surrender

A combination of guided imagery, breathing techniques and music.
Side one instructional.
Side two mainly music.
Relaxation techniques that can improve your emotional and physical sense of well being. Aid to better sleeping and living life more fully in the moment.

The Gift of Laughter

The laughter of children mingled with the music of a babbling brook. Just plain old fun, helping to rekindle the child within.

Order Form

BOOKS	Qty	Price	Total
The Make Love With Life Journal over 100 inspirational & motivational sayings		$9.95	
222 Ways to Make Love With Life How To Love, Laugh and Live in the Moment		$9.95	
222 More Ways to Make Love With Life More Ways for Living in the Moment		$9.95	
For Lovers Only 222 Ways to Enhance the Magic		$9.95	
222 Ways to Stress Free Living Reduce Stress and Make Love With Life		$9.95	
The Ultimate Power How to Unlock Your Mind Body Soul Potential		$14.95	
AUDIO TAPES			
The Ultimate Power – 8 cassettes program includes the book		$89.95	
Hypnotic Journey of Gentle Surrender – Relaxation techniques		$14.95	
The Gift of Laughter helping to rekindle the child within		$14.95	
Special Offer – all audio tapes Save over $20 now!		$99.00	
	Sub-total		
(over $36 free delivery or $3.00 for 1st item + $0.50 for each additional item) Shipping			
	Total		

Name_____

Address _____

City _____ZIP _____

Phone _____

Please make certified check/money order payable to and send to
Adi, Gaia, Esalen Publications Inc.
8391 Beverly St. #323-ML, Los Angeles, CA 90048

VISA ❑   MasterCard ❑   American Express ❑
Call Toll free 1-800-263-1991
Overseas call (519) 396-9553 or Fax (519) 396-9554

About the Author...

Ken Vegotsky

...is a professional speaker, author and entrepreneur. Ken has given keynote addresses and seminars in the U.S.A. and Canada. He has been featured in print, radio and TV in the U.S.A., Canada, Australia, New Zealand, United Kingdom and a host of other countries.

"Ken is the Victor Frankl of our day," noted Dottie Walters, President of Walters Speakers Bureau and author of *Speak & Grow Rich*.

Mark Victor Hansen, New York Times #1 best-selling co-author of the *Chicken Soup for the Soul*, says Ken's work is, *"Brilliant and Illuminating."*

"In recognition of being seen as a model of courage and hope for others, who demonstrates to all of us the nobility of the human spirit..." begins the Clarke Institute Psychiatric Foundation nomination of Ken for a *Courage To Come Back Award*. These awards were originated by the St. Francis Health Foundation of Pittsburgh, PA.

Ken has served on the boards of NACPAC (affiliate of the American Chronic Pain Association) and a half-way home for mentally challenged people in transition. After numerous inspirational speeches, Ken was encouraged by listeners to tell his story.

His National Bestseller, *The Ultimate Power* shares his captivating first-person account of his near-death experience, garnished with proven keys for unlocking your personal power.

Discover *How to Make Love With Life*™. You'll feel embraced by caring and compassion as you share his moving experience.

To arrange a keynote, seminar and/or workshop presentation by Ken Vegotsky call the contact coordinator at (519) 396-9553.